Easy Space Definitions Astronomy Picture Book for Kids

Astronomy & Space Science

BABY PROFESSOR

EDUCATION KIDS

Speedy Publishing LLC
40 E. Main St. #1156
Newark, DE 19711
www.speedypublishing.com

Some terminology used by astronomers in studying the universe can be confusing if you haven't met the word before.

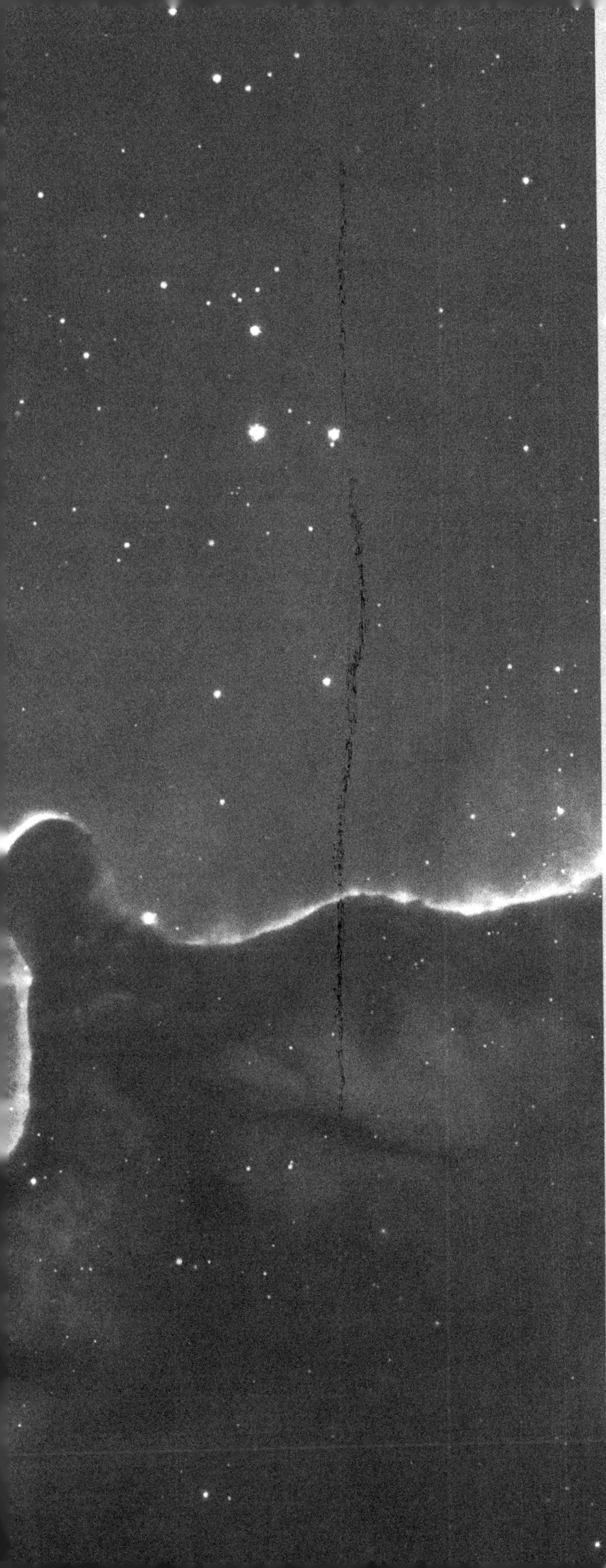

Knowing the different terms used in astronomy helps broaden our knowledge about the universe.

Andromeda Galaxy

It is a spiral galaxy also known as Messier 31 or M31. This galaxy can be found in the Andromeda constellation and is the neighboring spiral galaxy of the Milky Way. Its distance from Earth is 2.5 million light years. An estimated one trillion stars can be found in the galaxy.

Asteroid

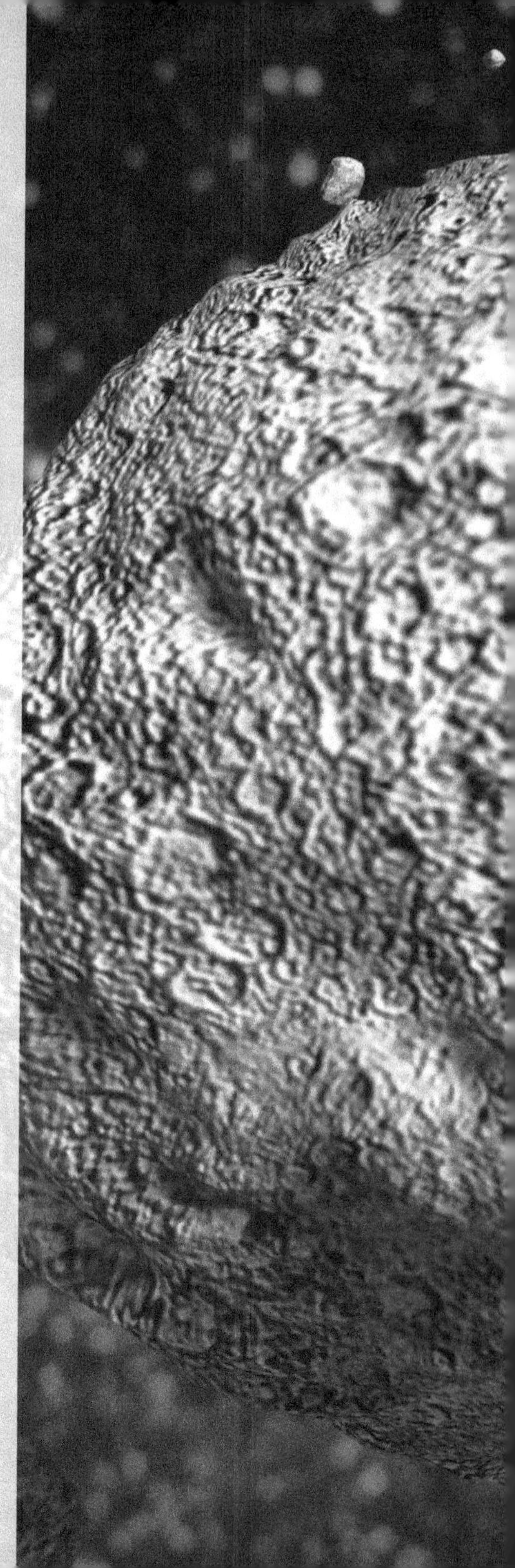

A small body of rock that orbits around the Sun. It is larger than a meteor but is smaller than a moon or a planet. Most of the asteroids are located between the planets Mars and Jupiter. Their size ranges from 1.6 kilometer (less than one mile) to 775 kilometers. Asteroids are also known as minor planets.

Astronomy

It is the study of stars, the Sun, moons, comets, galaxies, planets, and other objects beyond the Earth's atmosphere. Astronomy was first treated as a branch of mathematics by the ancient Greeks.

Big Bang Theory

A scientific theory about how the universe began from a huge explosion that happened 13.7 billion years ago. It is currently the accepted theory for the origin of the universe. This theory came from observations by Edwin Hubble that the universe is continuously expanding.

Black Hole

It is a place in space where the force of gravity is so strong that not even light can escape. Some dying stars can lead to black holes and they come in different sizes. Black holes are invisible and only space telescopes with special tools can locate them.

Comet

A comet is a small celestial body that orbits the sun just like the planets. Its center (nucleus) is made of ice and dust. When it gets near the sun, it produces a tail of gas and dust. Its orbit around the Sun is a very long oval, so it comes close to the Sun and then travels far, far away before returning.

Dark Energy

An unknown or unidentified form of energy in space with a force that opposes gravity and affects the accelerating expansion of the universe. Around 68% of the universe is made of dark energy.

Dark Matter

It is a matter that cannot be seen in the universe. Dark matter is roughly 27% of the universe. It doesn't produce light or energy but it can be detected through its gravitational effects. It was first identified by Fritz Zwicky at Caltech in 1933.

Galaxy

A collection of stars and their solar systems, gas, and dust. The force that holds together a galaxy is gravity. Some galaxies are elliptical, irregular, and spiral. Their size ranges from dwarf (less than a billion stars) to giant galaxies (one hundred trillion stars).

Kuiper Belt

Bits of rock, ice, comets, and dwarf planets can be found in the Kuiper Belt, which is located outside of Neptune's orbit. Objects that can be found in the Kuiper Belt are known as Kuiper Belt Objects or KPO, and the most famous object floating in the belt is the dwarf planet Pluto. It is named after the scientist Gerard Kuiper.

Meteor

It is a piece of rock that burns and vaporizes, making a bright glow in the sky, as it reaches the Earth's atmosphere. Meteors are also known as shooting stars.

Milky Way

It is the galaxy that includes our solar system. The center of the Milky Way is full of stars, gas, and dust. An estimate of 100-400 billion stars and at least 100 billion planets can be found in the galaxy. There is a big black hole in the center of the galaxy.

Refractor

The earliest type of optical telescope that uses lenses instead of mirrors to gather light. It is used to see the moon and the planets, but the result of a refractor is not as detailed as from a reflector.

Supernova

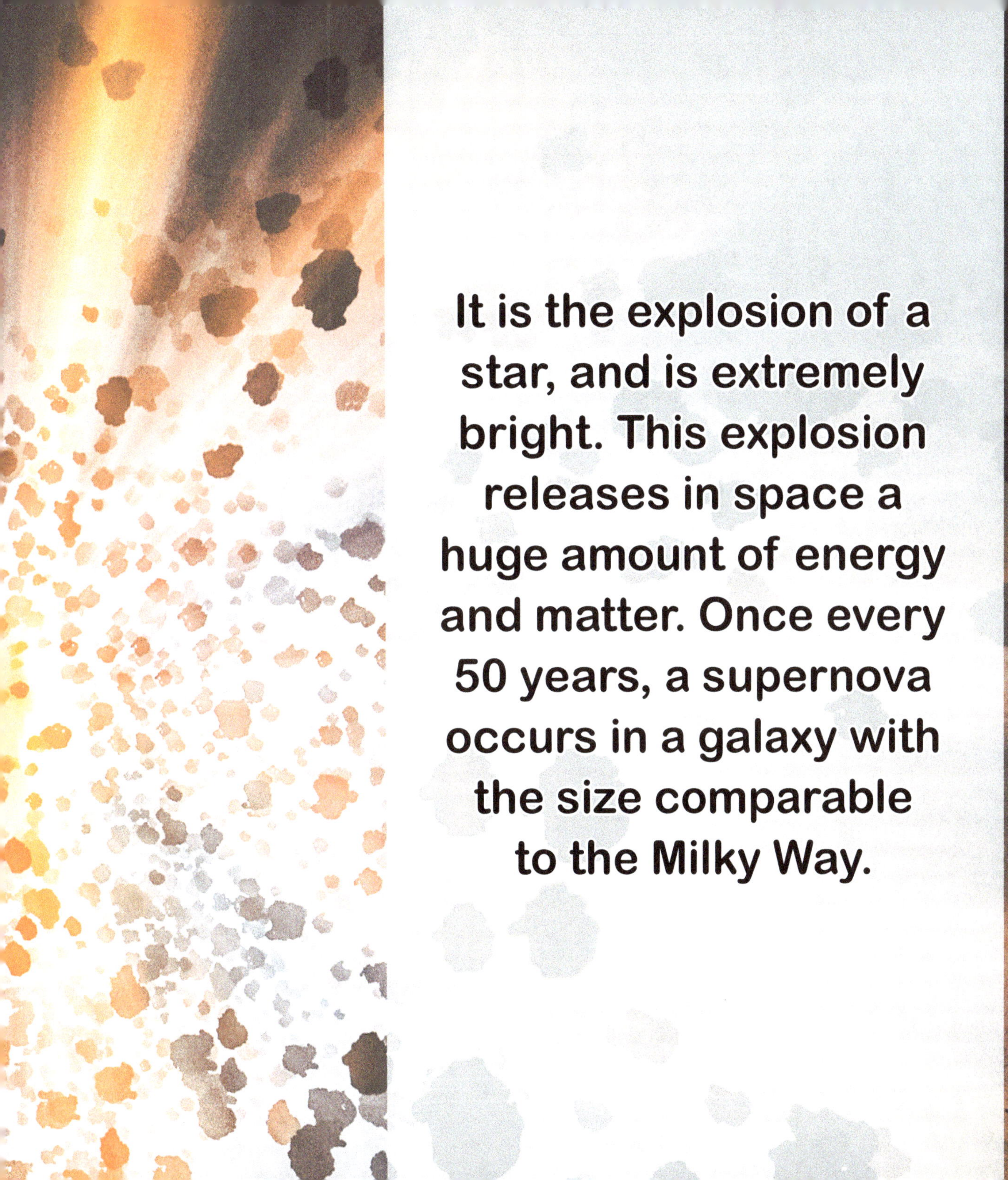
It is the explosion of a star, and is extremely bright. This explosion releases in space a huge amount of energy and matter. Once every 50 years, a supernova occurs in a galaxy with the size comparable to the Milky Way.

There are more
space astronomy
terms. Research
more and have fun!

Visit

BABY PROFESSOR
EDUCATION KIDS

www.BabyProfessorBooks.com
to download Free Baby Professor eBooks
and view our catalog of new and exciting
Children's Books